Laughing Africa

Winner of the Iowa Poetry Prize

Poems by Terese Svoboda

* * * * * * * * * *

Laughing Africa

University of Iowa Press Ψ Iowa City

University of Iowa Press, Iowa City 52242
Copyright © 1990 by Terese Svoboda
All rights reserved
Printed in the United States of America
First edition, 1990

Design by Richard Hendel

*Library of Congress
Cataloging-in-Publication Data*
Svoboda, Terese.
Laughing Africa: poems/by Terese
Svoboda.—1st ed.
    p.   cm.—(The Iowa poetry prize)
ISBN 0-87745-280-6 (alk. paper),
ISBN 0-87745-272-5 (pbk., alk. paper)
I. Title.   II. Series.
PS3569.V6L3   1990   89-20520
811'.54—dc20   CIP

Grateful acknowledgment is made to the
following publications in which some of
these poems first appeared: *Paris Review,
Pequod, Pennsylvania Review, Virginia
Quarterly Review, Ploughshares, Chelsea,
Prairie Schooner, Tar River Poetry, New
England Review/Bread Loaf Quarterly,
Manhattan Poetry Review, Denver
Quarterly, 5 A.M., Columbia, Gettysburg
Review, Massachusetts Review, American
Poetry Review, Boulevard, New Yorker,*
and *Yale Review.* The author also wishes
to thank the Corporation of Yaddo.

Printed on acid-free paper

To Anne Marie Walsh Svoboda

and Carolyn Stoloff

Publication of this book was made

possible by a generous grant from

the University of Iowa Foundation

Contents

*   *   *

I

II

III

I

*   *   *   *   *   *   *   *   *   *

Laughing Africa

*　　*　　*　　*

Nights in the barn, the clean astringence of urine
steaming into the tendrils of a dungfire, the cattle

sleeping their own way, and me mine, despite the puppies
tied to the housepost, their lean mother snapping, the only window

stuffed with straw. *To keep out snakes?*
No. Reic shifts at watch.

To block the cuckold's spear from the lover's heart.
But once I hear low-flying planes and once a helicopter

comes chop-chopping over this basket of a barn
and Reic lifts his ancient rifle, practically

a blunderbuss, and says, *Of course bullets come right through.*
I imagine seeing his wife's breast bleed as she runs,

the wisps of straw catching fire, the lover, Reic,
his children running slant into the suddenly windy savannah.

There is this laugh that Reic makes, the time he finds
a guerrilla stuffed inside a dead cow. *How could you do this?*

he laughs, *I have so many to feed. Couldn't you hide*
behind some bush instead of the stomach of my cow?

And then he roars, and the strength of it is the measure
of his misfortune. Today Reic and all the people who fed me

are starving, the last Red Cross plane just now downed,
every passenger shot. But what's two million Sudanese?

Nothing to you. To me, it's Reic's clasp multiplied—
not diminished to facelessness, or the archetype of a Grimm tale,

it's Nyapuok rubbing her back with sand, Nyabel grinding grain,
sinuous against rock and water, little Lam checking my breasts

for color, Pel singing to his sister, and that laugh,
that laugh. True, they only fed me once a day,

but it was their only meal. And even if it were the last
fowl beaten from the bush by a string of hungry children,

I ate it. My hunger was the first inescapable experience
I'd ever had, mine and no other's. I sucked the stones

of the tamarind and felt lucky, and the touch of malaria
that shook the food off my spoon, and the diarrhea

turned dysentery that drove me away, with excuses, midmeal,
and whatever it was that hurt the gut even when I did eat

(was it worms? the kind you sugar a cut for so they come
crawling out of the wound?) were only the discomforts

of the initiate, the stupid. *What kind of snake was it?*
I point to the black foot of a man already black.

4

Not poisonous, he says, limping into the sunset,
if I live till morning. And he laughs, walking into

a bloody horizon clean of everything, even the stumps of trees,
and it is not that he dies but that his figure grows smaller.

The Greeks were almost African.

*

I hear Africa singing, sable and onyx,
chants in a language more alien to me

than even Homer's, and what I see is Africa
the beautiful, a wildness that's America's

no longer, its light the one photographers
call blessed, its plains still purple

to the earth's core, its arid canyons split
like skulls for man's first upright grasp.

Atrocities in the Garden of Eden?
As if nudity made people simpler

or children sweetened the limepit.

*

There is no translation for *machinegun*
and what they use is not pidgin. In the bush

the smallest boys spit on clay replicas,
metal-black and shiny, and then shoot rounds

of wet stinging nettle at each other,
like our children. And in the dusk, one young man asks:

Are you my bride? The CIA promised me a woman.
I don't ask what he did, what betrayal warranted such reward.

What I do know is that there's oil under Wau,
though UPI reports the slaughter's North vs. South, Black/Arab.

Oil instead of slaves, both *ultra vires*,
worth any number of lives. Ten years ago men met

in a clearing and bashed each other over the head with clubs,
causing no casualties. We sold the guns,

and like the British, whose Sheffield steel
made a fortune selling tomahawks,

we too may reap in coarse design
as in a film from Niger, where Africans disembark

Pan Am in cowboy costume and Marilyn Monroe truck
and re-create the panoply of us and them to ask:

Why do you wear clothes if not to hide your guns?

*

For them, children are the only immortality.
6 Mothers walked forty miles thinking me a nurse,

and spit at my trivial interest in their songs.
But we don't believe in children;

they are *had* like chickenpox, and gotten over.
Nor do we believe in immortality,

a juvenile pre-Freudian fixation,
nor in the pleasure of living every day

for the pleasure of it. We believe work makes us safe,
or love, some four-letter word.

Oh, the women are laughing now, their children
light in their arms. I can imagine

my own little Felix, all his four years
and heavy big-boy boots, in my arms, swallowing,

swallowing—but the empathy stinks,
goes coy with metaphor, evades by fingering, by taming the horror

into mere minutes of my time. I know nothing.
Out in their dark, the real dark without a moon

or anything electrical, comes lightning as long as the Nile,
and it silences the milling hungry people,

the way it used to when I bore witness.
The ants of god they call themselves.

What does that make me?

Captain Andy

*   *   *   *

Leave me be. From here on the veranda
I watch a path that's not slimed by slugs,
or soiled by rabbits, the damn brown rabbits
pausing in their gnawing, or the high stink
of daisies, but one that's combed sand, palm, crab.

What light there is mottles my hands into
sealskin, dumb critters I killed for a time,
so merrily. With just a tap, their chops
turned quite violet, a singer's color.
Not me, nor my wife, Ngarima, could sing,

though her lovetunes—whew! Crescendo, I heard
them call it, real crescendo. To me, she's
"Anemone" for how her legs flail. Why
do words at the end get better? Shouldn't
they get stuck up in the pump as it rusts?

In this light I'm on my boat, a swan's back.
That's the English in me, the swan. Better
a re-fined shark. Like all sailors, I hate
the water and anything in it.
First time I clippered was after flogging

Victoria's death. Oh, a boat in black,
crack-silent, the sailors doffed—there's the soul.
Then I weathered a grand typhoon. Too young
for women (begging your pardon), I drank
double rum as we wallowed down. Since that

wasn't the end, I changed. After suchlike
some men float in their eye juice, tide to tide.
Only a stirring in the groin tricked me
into coming about, my Ngarima.
She's a strong wind, she filled me. We traded

a schoonerful of string, hooks, lemon drops.
Might as well as been the goddamn family
ferry since we stuck to ports with sisters
and grass huts. I went fat as a porpoise
on good bream. But this is no life story;

there's a point, that these Poly-nesians
sail to the pull of their balls, not string maps.
That's all cat's cradle. And their balls are wrong.
How often I've hauled them in! They laughed when
I stuck my hand in the sky as if to

hold on. The right stars always steered my dreams,
so the booming at midnight was the reef
and not the bottom of the boat, a sound
as sickening as a child's night cough.
Stars bored into me as I humped on deck

with all the lamps off or got tied to the mast,
for penance. This is why the bed's out here.
I got to see my way. Change sixty years
of star-towing just for a little dying?
Put out the light. I can smell their burning.

The Dead Dance

*   *   *   *

The winds were headed straight at us
for days before and during the test.
—Glen Curbow, former Rongerik
    weather unit commander for BRAVO,
    the largest of the 300 H-bombs
    exploded over the Pacific

I

Polynesia seemed just a fifth-grade
dalliance in sticky crepe paper or,
at most, the prom's promise, an upright fan
blowing against a cardboard palm,

when I flew there, so hip to the sixties'
four-letter love that the two men
caught coupling in the plane's john
merely amused me. But that first morning,

waking not only to the ardent rooster
but to two goats soldered
to each other, then changing
money, the prim Queen on one side

Tangaroa on the other, all member,
then blocked from breakfast
by a parade where the figure
on the float pumped watery milk

all over the cheering crowd,
I clutched at my pills.
Too dazzled by sex for promiscuity,
still learning *a* to *b*

memorizing the *Kama Sutra*,
my education wasn't that Catholic.
"You stinky vagina!" one kid shouted
to another. "You bent penis!"

While one's first translations
aren't always the most profound,
preoccupations tell: Eskimos, snow;
Africans, cows; Americans, cars.

"The back of the rat goes up and down."
The P.M.'s son, a darker Charles Laughton,
is his brother's father. This,
what we call the last husk, shucked.

II

Ah, the noble savage who is
neither. I go dancing that night.
Rather, I buy a drink and the women's
swaying raffia advances on me,

the drumming men turn all insistence,
daring me to do what all my adolescent
"jerks," "dirty dogs," "limbos"
had not prepared me for. Oh, no.

Circle by circle, my crude motions
lose all innocence, and they
laugh, mimic me, laugh again.
But it's the song that suggests

more depth: "Pan America,"
named after the plane
that burned over Tahiti,
dancer-full. A twitching

sadness it is, in a slightly minor
key, a tragedy to dance to.
We yell at the end, touched,
erotic, thankful.

III

Palms broom the yard, flailing
with spray that's more than rain,
a typhoon's air-and-ocean.

Two chickens fight for shelter
under a pawpaw. Whichever wins is dinner.
Ngarima twirls her machete until the storm's

all fluff, and out of this haze zigzags
Preacher Vatu in a football helmet.
He raps his knuckle against its vinyl:

"Coconuts in this wind can kill you."
We sip hot tea on our haunches
as the chicken grills but he won't wait

to eat. "A miscarriage to attend."
He tips his head toward the mountain.
"Before, I didn't bother."

Out beyond the pawpaw stands the fence,
every inch flowers. Here, where a twig drops,
there's a tree tomorrow.

IV

Polynesia's ghosts are not forgotten.
At night even the dogs howl for their kind,

roasting in the *umu*, cut down in packs
by cars, the island's thinnings.

I almost miss their smokeless oven,
walk over one and think it's only clots

of pulsing lava. The ghosts of humans seep
from nearby broken crypts, the limestone

paper-flimsy against hibiscus or the thick
poison roots of manioc. The dead

must dance, one moon-gold boy
insists. I witness a funeral:

begun in propriety, matching dresses,
dark slacks, white shirts, straw hats,

then someone sings, and by the chorus
two women are doing pew-side what to them

is pure offering, to us, lust. The spiritual
can never equal the scent of *tipani*,

a blood-heat climate, the body's pleasure,
a glide across a plate-flat lagoon.

Once you die, you're as good as a radio
left out in the rain or a cassette unstrung—

hardly rewarded. No, the dead want back
and those athwart the graves, coupling

under canopies of mats, try to persuade them
otherwise, crying out over love-thrusts.

V

But a miscarriage mourned?
Here everyone gets a baby, even
single young men, largesse from women

with over ten, *succès d'estime.*
It is amusing, that primitive measure.
More than amusing. Vili twists

a teenager's arm so I can see the marks.
"I make some tests to stop the babies.
I tell them Be modern, it's like Coke,

this vaccination. When I finish
I get a ticket to Switzerland, land
of leather shorts. Can you believe it?"

All for me, for some new packet of birth control.
For that each woman's promised an equivalent mirror
or matches, TV or stove,

for a month's barrenness. Or more.
They don't know. I leave after six months
with reasons not as recondite

as Bligh's. "Paradise?
That went out with colonial
appellation, New this, New that,"

says some soured missionary
in the museum. In front of me,
every Tangaroa's penis-less.

VI

Ten years after the airport
farewell, the sports team singing
as their ladies shushushed
their skirts to "Pan America,"

I'm so much smarter.
I know the miscarriage was a jelly baby,
one of many born in secret,
with transparent twitching organs only,

or worse, a live monster with rolling
eyes, few limbs, half-human cries,
some women now with seven tries.
Think Krakatoa,

that Polynesian Apocalypse, that atoll
explosion that gave Europe
its first sunset beauty, the decor
for Mann's beaches, a fin de siècle

ornament, then think bigger, think
BRAVO, that American self-congratulation
twenty-five miles high planned
to test the people of Paradise,

then three hundred more mushrooms
cracking the atolls, dusting
the children in yellow, burning spore.
Instead of milkspray from a homemade god,

the half-life of a juggernaut, ON
THE BEACH on the beach. Sold
to protect hot showers, Mercedes,
above-ground swimming pools,

and our new babies.
Yes, ours have finally arrived,
the "boom" of this generation
of equal size, our dalliance with sex

only a decade's fad. I know
so much more now. Such as:
how the sunset bleeds the world over,
how the palms bend at that hackneyed angle

with the same breeze that sways
the willows over Hackensack,
how the waves carry the wastes to me,
how they're all our babies.

No Historical Marker

*　　*　　*　　*　　*

An anthropologist takes us to the
highest point of Waiheke Island,
New Zealand.

"Anything high, to quote Eliade, hooks up
to God. But," she says, "there's also
the intoxication of subjugation,

if only the meadow to the mountain.
This gigantic midden of oyster shell, fishbone,
and ash—trash, really—they called *pa*."

We climb it. Surely some jadeslung Maori,
nobly romantic or at least strong
from heaving boulders over the edge,

lifts us to his feathered shoulders:
It's exactly that high. The vista's
two more islands, the serifs

of twenty flagged sailboats,
the ripples of whales, a rosary of sheep.
We whoop: "This is paradise."

To that, birds crash through the low ferns
ingloriously, scandalizing their species
but trilling an apology so musical

it's obvious why they're spared extinction.
Then one fern goes on fluttering.
"It's the little people—a race

felled (like Ireland's) by clubs,
a harvest maybe a jot more humane
than that of jeans and pubs."

The fright pulls us down the side,
flapping like the birds weighting
the trees, already aroost in the dusk.

"Christ," she says, pouring tea,
"why should it be the moa that
haunts visitors the most?"

Color

*   *

I

My hands are like leaves,
you think. The worthless
surf dandles them. What?
The tide's on its way,

and it's day, not night,
the night that sucked
the mostly plastic plane
apart. You must move.

You must never move
the victim of an accident.
You move. Your head hurts
like you've downed

a whole drawerful
of miniature bottles.
You turn left, then right,
your neck at all angles.

Angels. The boy's not here,
nor husband. Water swirls up,
upchucks nothing but a shoe,
yours. "Mine," you say,

and there's no echo
from the white brochure
perfection spread out
around you.

you dream, yes,
you still do,
of boiling sails,
a petticoat found tied

to a palm in good shape,
except for the lace.
"Obeah!" you sing in sorrow.
She shucks oysters, she guts

grouper but it's as if
you're not there. All you want
is the answer to:
Where'd you come from?

Instead, you sit for months
without a fire.
"Animals have no fire,"
you tell Obeah.

III

Where'd you come from?
You see her ticketed,
walking through the electro-
magnetic portals,

her K Mart bags
cascading through the X ray.
Belted in, she divines the plane's
a slave ship:

there's the rationed food,
the parroted preparations
for disaster, passengers
in dazed bas-relief.

Then the imagined plane
splits open and out she steps,
gossamer blowing
in her face. Or is it rags?

"My hands are like yours."
Now she reaches toward you,
white palm up. You realize then
she's your photographic reverse,

the anti-you, opposed
and terrible. What ensues
is this great sexual
bust so primitive, so elemental,

so subatomic—she blows up.
Crisp bones, crisp hide.
Chitterlings.
You loved her, you don't eat her.

Where'd you come from?
You do not, despite terraces
and potsherds, possess the world.
You talk to birds and when

they fall out
of the chromium sky,
you eat them, fat
for a week on false

providence, then die.
By that time,
the plane's sanded
wing glitters like

a dragonfly's
and the scientists
in white face
are due to arrive.

Komodo Dragon

*   *   *   *

You can get there only from Kuala Lumpur, not Timor.
No one's left in Timor since we exterminated them
    in '74,
         the masked invasion only a minor inconvenience
    to air travelers to Bali,
one which left no survivors but what they call "pirates,"
         people who once had homes and thieves of their
         own.

No survivors. Once on Komodo, you'll see the dragons,
saved from god-knows-what interplanetary winter
    of casual radiation.
        They wallow in hot estuaries
    but do not spew fire.
Man had to invent that, unable to accept how
        the term *cold-blooded* wedded us.

I'm thinking now of the Tasmanians, other island-dwellers.
When the English landed, those proto-anthropologists,
    justice lovers,
        and Benthamites, they slaughtered all
    but ten of them. The survivors sat
for a photo wearing borrowed spats and leg-o'-muttons,
        looking like Cro-Magnon acceding to Homo
        Sapien.

In Komodo, the Japanese men with their long lenses seem voyeuristic
in intent and the bleak quonset huts with their orange
    and green plastic
           dragons, casts of footprints,
        photos of various half-eaten
carcasses, minus the flies, prepare one
                for similar cheapness.

But at 120 degrees and every inch beyond the blind
teeming with hand-wide spiders, vipers with beige eyes,
    and double-tined
           nits dragging proboscis elephant-size,
        one demands more than special effects.
And the animal (reptiles are still
           animals) rewards. Its feeding, that tear

and rip and gulp, is esctasy—who could forget
the low hiss, the avian skittering,
    the delicate
           tasting, touching, smelling tongue,
        how it alarmed one, especially this last,
like a nervous predilection, or worse,
             a licking of the lips.

Yards of innards float forth, almost out of view,
that of a pony, or some surprised sleeping native,
    and cockatoo
           cruise the offal
        with sea eagles, and friar birds.
Half the dragon's life is bird's, lounging in the lontar
             palm until its weight breaks the nearly hollow
             tree.

Then it trots back through the bush and digs burrows.
Until 1912 no one knew they existed.
    That is,
               no one who counted, meaning
          no white. Imagine the dragons swimming up,
the researcher at his washing . . .
                  And how they survived when others died

is all mystery. Most likely they just drifted
along on their crack of land, their persistence
     as undirected
          as ours will be,
        given our propensity to let things slide.
Mutation, that's the ticket.
               We'll have a dream about Raymond Burr

skeptical of Godzilla's arrival amid
the nuclear rubble and then wake up
    to find
           what we're dying of
       is not the usual cancer, that we're just growing
more arms, all of us well on our way
              to becoming Shiva.

Or Kali. Would bestiality be better?
With dragons? More likely roaches—
    they're
          the more secure species.
    I think I'd prefer
cloning, some Kafka solution, the hard shell exterior,
          something simple inside.

The dragon grows to six feet and weighs more than
the great Jackie Gleason.
    We worship what awes us, and
           though we relegate gigantism
      to ancient Greeks and Fat Boy Burgers,
this slip of overgrown prehistory,
          these fewer than one thousand dragons, counting

even the newt-sized newborns from the nests
of thirty-six, keeps us shuddering
    for our own specialness,
      for something
    to ward off pirates and merchants.
We are lucky, however, to believe everything wild
        tastes like chicken, except ourselves.

Water Ballet

*   *   *

Fat black flies looking for milk
to sink into, that noise, the dropping
past the meniscus, that dipping
of the swimming cap in unison,
that constellation of the feminine,

the sleek heads so seal-like. (I've held
a grey infant in my arms in a Safeway
parking lot. It put up its face
for stroking, a deep sound running up
its fur jowls, a fish-purr.

It died in someone's bathtub, butting
its head on the edge, flailing
its flippers like an amputee.)
When the women let their hair free to float
in circlets around their faces,

the synchronicity recreates an old-fashioned
favorite: the loose strands of a bracelet
around some mourner's wrist,
as in Gretchen's case, a girl rehearsing
for an Olympics, blonde though Rosenberg

in the Weimar, and in perfect formation,
the suck and dive effortless to the bland chords
of accordions inhaling and exhaling their little triumphs,
her four limbs spewing into the air by themselves,
while twenty other women backfloat the bloom of a rose.

Cowboy

*   *   *

The rez was a strip of light
I'd hitchhiked not far enough into.
Already the stubble held the down
of the next snowfall and the moon's

albumen, and no one drove by.
Until, like the opening shot where a car
seems to float in one place, it came,
unspooling in size, not one rise

between us, just sky. I jumped up
and down on the middle line to stop
those fifteen Sioux in a coupe,
a carnival ride. They had room.

But what they had left of their names
was all fake: John Steele,
Henrietta Sells, and Sean, the baby,
whose mouth kept kissing the air.

Was Moon-in-the-Hair better?
Or Yellow Snake? Oliver, the squinter,
a speeder, our driver, took up talking:
"I was ten, old enough to be done

playing Indian." "Whoever done?"
sang someone in reprise from the backseat.
We all laughed. Oliver knocked
the wipers on. "My brother Albert"—

the name shushed them all—"showed me
how to tie the knot, the knot
for the lynching part. I was the one
who hauled up the rope, the only one

big enough." A handful of snow blew
up from the vent. "Well, somebody
had to be cowboy." We slid off
the road a ways, hitting ice,

then slid back. "Some say Indians
got nothing. I say we got a load.
To die a white man's death . . ."
He shook his head. "In Nam,

I shot a kid in the face
who had a grenade tied to his waist
and his face was Albert's.
That time I knew

what I did, or thought so.
But I waited too long." He popped out
one fake blue eyeball and handed it,
woman by woman, to me. "Next time

I kill for whitey, it had better be
suicide." He giggled away, steering
with his chest, opening the sixth
of a six-pack. I couldn't complain.

He took me clear into dawn,
to a truckstop where I could see,
over coffee, halfway across the state,
how snow lay over most of it.

Beyond Borders

*   *   *   *

Chile had been cleanly filleted as yet another CIA
plot, ho-hum after Watergate, and absolved in history
by the movies, and Central America was still the sleepy
sombrero, despite Cuba, gem-setted by the bright bananas
of Asturias against vibrant ghosts, swinging machetes

when Christian entered, the name embodying
a certain empathy with just, if not pacific, aims.
He took my older woman's hand and guided it to a member
all peninsular, then his English broke with emotion—
idolatry—and didn't sound corny. We met like convex

currents, producing spume and daze, the knots we rode
so fast obscured all we passed. And we passed some,
mostly jealous women he'd been seeing, my ex-husband
whom he shoved me toward, a test of course, but so hard
I fell into the street. All forgotten. Until one night,

four whiskies downed—drunk, I think, for courage—
he snapped off his safe, a sound like chewing gum
exploding in the face and said what one man did,
he would too. I was territory, an isthmus in the way
of conquest. Though his upright thing enthralled me,

children were one tropics I'd been through. He growled,
his hard chest went from harbor to armor, leaving
my body atilt, wanting. He forgot
his sweater so I put it on, my confusion of tears
drycleaning his scent. Then I telephoned, dazed.

"Wife, wife, wife," he whispered, unasked,
totally non sequitur. I should have known,
but a lover loves—the words were right. What I answered
did not suffice. "If you say that again (what? what?)
I'll knock your teeth in." Still just words, still

between the loving plunge and sigh. It's cultural—
I'm not pronouncing properly or the noise he makes
blocks my loving answer. I don't feel coy. Or teasing.
Just old and getting older. None of my friends . . .
He introduces me to his mother, since wifecalling

requires that. Ringed and wigged and manicured,
she avoids my eyes but her examination
is total. *Pendejo*, she says, *Búscala*. He kisses her.
All he's witnessed: the police kicking in
his best friend's head; his father shaking in the closet;

what happened to his sister, his sister, his sister.
Yet what he wants most is a sports car. "Víctor Jara,"
I quizzed, "that severed hand strumming in the stadium?"
Ay, qué linda, I have it on record, *qué música*.

Days pass anyway. The elastic in my lingerie wears out
so I buy new—"a flag of cuckoldry," he sneezes, in fury.
He takes my head and cracks the wall with it.
"Say *sorry*." With that my brain clears.
I claw and bite and kick until he loosens his grip—

and he's smiling. "That's more like it."
It is. I call the police and in minutes
he's so sure of himself he returns for another round
of endearments. "Traitor," he screams, "traitor."
What one country won't do to another.

Slaughter of the Centaurs

*   *   *   *   *   *

Woods, glades, copses, massed oak,
the vines of Atreus, trillium,
dogbane, an excess of green,
the insects cryptic with cold,
green with a fine English

mist which softens the streaks
of blood glistening on the flanks
of the coarsely forelocked boys,
none more than fifteen,
beardless, death

catching them cantering,
berets cocked, weapons not.
See the tatoos on their chests,
the mermaid's swinging hair,
the laughing snake? They went

as we will. See the strong hooves
still twitching? The warm earth,
ravaged in reflex? But they were
warriors, planted in their mothers'
wombs for nothing else,

their beautiful tails curled
around their wet bellies,
lifted, so delicately, to fan
the light. Brighter now, you can see
boys in wrecked jeeps in camouflage.

Conquistador

*　　*　　*　　*

By June the vine takes the far wall,
each leaf's corpulence gored
as it falls in concaves, cupping
here a chipped brick, there a crevice
in molding, yet skittering up,
the shoot end hot white, divine,
the left behind bit dull
against the whitewashed (grey-)
spattered city wall.
Like an illuminated curlicue,
the vine provides, with grace,
importance.

The sky is generous all summer:
light stripes clear to my window
once, and spokes of pigeons reel the vine up
into the cloudlessness.
Affixed to this thicket,
a birdhouse pronounces its entrance *o* all day
but the birds hop past,
afraid, I think,
to re-emerge green-winged,
green-sighted
among the leaves.

Winter, the wind clatters through,
the leaves shieldshape, thin.
The Puerto Ricans sorting rags
across the airspace
jerk to their headphones:
one leg up, one down,
like the parrots
they've left behind
in a world abounding
with vines, vines
as green to the wall
as what binds them here
in the haze of the rags'
disintegration. Calendar-size,
they can't see
the still-bright leaves below,
a tropic swathed in ice,
more flesh than ever before.

Nothing Beautiful except in Things

*   *   *   *   *   *   *

He is green with screen. The machine
takes his etch-a-sketch to the nth pixel,
a branching more numinous than Godlight
and just as postulated. He's used to the edge

though, space purdah, the lover's ache
all chrome, tumbling to the stars,
no one touching no one, and none to see
past that grille

        to the boy playing with matches,
his face ecstatic each time the flame flames—
that, sealed in plastic—as Columbus
would have become sails if he could

in the libido of experiment. Ironically enough,
the soul is what he means by body now,
the axials of the waving hand reduced
to screws, and the ephemera: the unregulated

tic, the famed fuzzy logic is as chemical
as passion or hypochondria. To this, he strews
the chips from previously simple elements,
our carbon heritage, briefing the gold calf

for the resurrection, the winging of computers
toward an angle in space. Meanwhile we reverence
the plug, its relief, for who controls it
is still the guerrilla of the heavens, and divine.

Do Machines Bleed?

＊　　＊　　＊　　＊　　＊

Posit headlights as a form of intelligence.
They cut the dark into discrete parallels.

Pick any car. Its shadow stamps it
MADE IN REALITY yet allows for confusion,
the sun's place, the motor's size and shape.

Travel, too. Why, this tower
could be holding the waters of India, not
Long Island. Travel lulls us into thinking

maybe it is or could be. Take the Japanese,
the most Toyota of us all. They wave until
their visitors are completely out of sight.

The same intelligence asks: do machines bleed?
But question the tangible and they lock you up
for seeing parallels.

Instead, tell stories.
Once there was a mermaid.
She washed up in a storm
and cried and cried until
her tears became a conductor
for kisses.

Some were witnesses.
Some still talk about it:
how the mermaid was locked in the minister's bathroom
and what she did to escape.
They found evidence of pleasures
they'd never imagined.

So they talked and talked
and the talk ended up being
more than the mermaid, more than
a story of enchantment,
the way the talk of love
transforms itself from an ache
into the soft flip of a fish
coming aboard.

Later generations believed
the mermaid was all a trick of sight,
a sleight of hand, a story.

But she was always there,
like a principle of science:
what keeps airplanes up,
what makes a chip transmit.

And like the best principles,
this is the beginning,
not the end, we return
by any means,
the birds fly back with branches,
and the night takes on
its parallels.

II

*　*　*　*　*　*　*　*　*　*

The Ranchhand's Daughter

*   *   *   *   *   *

I

Not even the Indians who worshiped land
could abide this blank territory; they shunned
it, left bears' bones at its perimeter.
Blasting the presidents' faces in made
for a helluva slide, tourists, exits
lined with arches framing Ozymandian
reaches. When herds die in these ravines, no one
notices until spring when snowmobiles
whine, flipping over the gopher holes, landing
upright. And if sometimes stories circulate
about big spreads and the ranchhand's daughter,
it's only the Badlands seeking substance.
With its goddess rising from a shell sunk
in the ooze of lost natural gas, with flames
obviously next, like scarves when the wind
whips up, which it always does, the land swims
against the sun, against the unending
anonymous roll of the hills, perfect
for the innocent goddess, the hulking
he-god, the forever-kneeling supplicant.

II

Junco, meadowlark, warbler, hawk burst up
out of the sagebrush like a backshuffled
card deck as she drove forward with nothing
for a road. She didn't know better, the web
of interstate thinned forty miles beyond
their three sections and the county seldom
fixed washouts. Her Chevy pickup took drops
the way a horse would, solemn and picky.
Right where the Lazy Y creekbed lent view
to the gully, canyon really, the walls ran
red yellow blue green welts along the side.
At eighteen, beauty bursting from her, she
knew only the grimy eyeletted moon
hanging a foot out of the trash dump.
Her wheels shivvied rock, then she tried to turn,
a couple of steers looked up, bothered, and
the salt lick in the back shifted so far
her front wheels left the ground, turning over.
To that, the radio popped on, the steers
drummed off, and all the birds in a mile hid.

III

Blair wasn't much of a nurse. He turned up
the heat, served spaghetti out of a can,
and killed flies. She didn't die. Doc Parks,
the vet, set the bones. He happened to see
the fire. Keep ice on her. You got ice? Blair
frowned Yes and the ranchhand fetched it. I'd have
her hauled out to the hospital despite
the trouble with her mother . . . Blair left
the room. Parks put a vial on the old bureau.
Ernie—the hand was back—These are for horses.
Tell Blair to half them before he feeds her.
And if she gets a fever, send for me.

She fevered. Blair took his car into town
and got drunk. She was in the talking sweats
when Ernie found her and made compresses
soaked in coffee. Didn't have no tea. After
he put out the feed, he sat by her bed
reading horoscopes in last week's paper.
Then, dreaming, there was her mother, alive,
sawhorse legs, double belly, cigarette
breath from smoking them up fast so she had
to go to town and going finally
out to the hospital cemetery
where for some reason a red cactus grew up
that never had to be watered. He woke.

IV

Once in a while Blair'll see the soddie.
The vetch is so high there you almost can't
get inside but you know when you're in it;
it's chilly and the wind stops. This last time
he could still hear the neighbor twenty miles
off in his spray plane. He shivered. The cold
made him feel in hell. Funny, being cold,
goodness kept in boxes of light set on
the floor. I'd like to start fresh, he thought, but
that would be fresh like fish, eyes clouded, gills
stinking, a smell for something living
too far away. I'd like to start—
It isn't for nothing I have her come
to me. They say the drop of a donkey
and a mule is worthless. I say it goes
back to horse. I want her mother, over
and over. All I have is need shaking
in my hands, a corner that I bite from,
backed into. Oh, wife. He spots the fake bronze
plaque the Duchess County Historical
Society put up saying this was
Jesse James' hideout when he laid low
disguised as a woman. Blair always felt
embarrassed by it. Before she was dead
his wife said You're past your time. You should
have a real gun, fine boots, and luck at cards.
He punched the two-foot-thick wall but didn't
do much. There's the mark, a clod short that side,
under the picture of the Virgin. Hey,
that's what it is. I'll be. The litho

54 fluttered. With one broad filthy finger he

smoothed it, then stood there in a daze, sensing
none of it would matter, having little
to do with either him or his daughter.

V

Only a slight rolling, the grey bedspread
rumpled, the chenille tufts pockets of sage
so spicy burnt that the ash had a taste.
Only a slight rolling generally,
the gully full of skulls, the sky bending
over a big blue backache. She's mended,
the horizon so far under her blind
pulling it down was an escape. Only
on Sundays they did no work and she hid.
Blair—why should she call him father?—stayed
waiting alone until he shouted for her.
She ran for the trap room once, in amongst
the spiked metal that smelled of rust and blood.
But he came for her. The hired hand played pool
just yards away in his bunkhouse or sat
in his naugahyde recliner fixing
harness or polished his pneumatic bow
and arrow. From his picture window
(the house being trailered from Ovid) lay
her car, still twisted. He would work on it,
but not Sundays he told her, he didn't like
being so close to the house then, though why
he never said, a dog's caution, maybe.

VI

Double eight ball over, sun in clover,
you're my lover or some such palaver
on the radio. The girl comes running,
the screen door banging over and over,
running as best she can with one leg still
screwed up out to the trap room which was strange,
given how much she hated that skinning
business, then Blair, coming after, but
hesitant, calling as if he didn't
really want to find her. Blair's wife used to
say, Ernie, you're gonna get curtains if
I have to use my old half slips. Of course,
real long ago. He turned from the window.
On the arm of his recliner he'd found
the girl's name scratched in, just yesterday he'd
seen it, watching TV, the rest of him
sleeping. Colt-legged she was when he'd come,
grizzled from too long on a road crew. When
she turned sixteen, and her father refused
to pay money to get her to high school,
he'd felt sorry. He'd found a coyote cub
and brought it in a box to her, leaving
it alongside the porch. But Blair found it,
slit its throat before she saw it. Good work,
Blair'd praised him, Got to get at them young.
Ernie'd nodded, took off the pelt, stuffed it
into a wall crack in his cold front room.

And she stumbled out sobbing.

VII

Mother, I lost the doll you once twisted
out of cornsilk for me. It was better
than Barbie. I still watch all the programs
you used to, and iron too. The sandcranes
still come in spring, so like the flapping birds
you made from newspaper, and storks too. Storks.
I was nine when you died, no baby but
not yet grown. You didn't say much except
that TV told some real bad fairytales.
We were sad about you together, Mom,
then just I was sad. But you often teased
Ernie, Dad says it, so I must come out
of a line of this type lady who likes
it. I'm sorry but I don't though. I like
catkins on my cheeks better, or nothing.
Yesterday I couldn't come visit you
because he hadn't yet. I love the square
with your name written in so the warblers can
pick at the june bugs that stray over
and the wind hollering down the slope
to where there's a real road and a place for
signs. I'm glad you're in the hospital lot
even if Dad says it's for bad women.

VIII

Mallards dive into the bright green custard.
Frogs lay their eggs in it, so thick they hatch
airborne and none escape the hungry ducks.
So few cows commence to drink from this spring
that the grass at its edges is a downy
green, a velveteen. She smoothes her hand
across it, expecting a stain. She's
never been here before, though she's driven
or walked far into her father's land. Slow
as a miracle asked for, the sun crops
a lone tree and the effort of the day
touches itself. She punches on the car
lights, holding the mirage before her like
jello over an oven, or moments
of television, then she turns toward stars
high enough in the horizon that they're
not fake and, keeping far from the dead cow
with calf mostly eaten, she drives straight home.

The horizon was what barred her. If she
put her hand up, she could grab it, if she
drove, there wasn't any way to get there.
School proved to be torture, a one-room–rule,
every kid as badassed as the bus that
brought them, and her, the farthest, five A.M.,
first stop, seven return, the last hour just
her and fat Mrs. Finstrom, the driver/
substitute who admired the cornsilk doll
she kept inside her jacket, once gave her
a pair of pantyhose and then died of
insulin shock, or, some of the bad kids
said, of overeating. No one came home
with her to play—but this was normal, she
didn't miss what she'd never had. Her breasts
budded, her majority came, eased in
by jeering classmates pointing to the spot,
singing out Apple butter, Apple butter.

When she started to fatten she ate less.
She unbuttoned her jeans, held them on with
rope, wore her blouses loose. Ernie caught her
saddling up, her scrawny arms high, her blouse
parting. Even he, motherless, with no
sisters, and a bachelor could see the foal
coming. That's something, he said. Your dad know?
She hid her eyes. No? You got to tell him.
He dragged her off the horse by her jean loops.
Who was it, he roared halfway to the house,
Leonard? A halfbreed selling satellite
dishes had come twice because she liked to

look at the pictures: aborigines
in Australia, spacemen in construction,
the dish a sort of hollyhock. Her dad
was with a sick cow both times so Ernie,
well, he sat and looked at the pictures too,
the first time, then couldn't take the repeat.
She shook her head while he shook her, then cowered:
He knows.
      He let go her arm.
            Pardon me.

X

For three months Ernie kicked silence around
like an old cow flop. He didn't move fast,
polished up his one bareback trophy and
the floor, clean enough to eat on. She swelled
like a two-door with a calf in the back.
Counting backward, Ernie ascertained that
Leonard was clear out of the county that
time, and wondered. Then in cold December,
the wind unforgiving, the cows bawling
in the feedlot, when changing the oil in
the pickup took forever, Ernie went
out to check on the cows. The heifers stood
on their heaped-up silage and, grape-eyed, stretched
their necks, bitterly ululant. Because
the cow-scratcher flapped loose from the barbed wire?
No, the trough under the windmill was why—
Blair face down in it like he was looking
to part his hair, and a power cord plugged
to the floodlights sizzling next to his head.
I said You wash up first. She had his shirt
on over her ripped-up nightie, and Blair
was nude. Behind her banged the loose wire, live,
smoking, an unstoppered halo. I don't
know nothing. Ernie climbed over the fence,
let the cows loose, slapping them fanny-wise.

XI

She delivered that day. Twisting his lips
the way he did when pulling calves, he watched.
The girl got wild and sobbing but didn't
beg for no one, not mother, and no man,
and cursed its sex as it delivered. Let it
strangle. But Ernie cut the cord and laid
the baby by her. Now, he said, we need
relief. He dialed up emergency, then
swept the house. She couldn't leave. She tried, trailing
afterbirth like a cat.

                   Sometimes they turn
themselves in, but Ernie? Really? Sheriff
Potts waived bail and even the unit loaned
from the capitol couldn't do much more
than fingerprint him again. No one had
an alibi. Who could stand as witness—
coyotes, cruising the rock-flecked range? She nursed
the baby through the inquest and wasn't
allowed to testify. Innocence sucked
in the silence. Perplexed, the judge deemed it
an accident, a man combing his hair,
nude, in winter, and a loose wire. She cried
then, shuddering, waking the baby.

The tractors didn't go for much, the cows,
once found, sold better, the auction drew more
than two hundred. People circled the trap
room and said what a fine-looking bride she
made, and how the little girl looked just like
her grandpa. But when Ernie showed up months
later to say she'd left for Montana,
that shocked them. All he had was the baby
and this dirty picture of the Virgin.

XII

And the ranchhand's so-called daughter? She grew
no way you'd think, raggy like the blue sage
even cows skip, not a tire tread against
drawn clouds, no John Deere beloveds rusting
heavenward. And she didn't grow wings to
satisfy whatever roan episode
myths shut on. She hunted for her mother
in more fertile quarter acres, and less,
in corn rows and pine forests, in lakes called
Mirror or Half Dollar, then she romanced
a park ranger to let her rappel down
the brow of one of those presidents. You
didn't read about it? Oh father, she
yelled, hugging him, I'm not afraid of falling.

III

＊　　＊　　＊　　＊　　＊　　＊　　＊　　＊　　＊　　＊

The Root of Mother Is Moth

*   *   *   *   *   *

At dusklight she slips
into acetate underclothing,
all rustling.

            Has she slept
all day? Or is that housedress
draped over the hassock warm? From her motion,
  one of submission, her pale arms
                    upraised, the slip sliding,
            talc issues invisibly.

Mother is faceless so far up in the dark.
Just her torso glows,
and the color around her takes on the design
of a falling leaf, grey-yellow plaid.

        From the mirror, she draws what little light
there is inside her, and sighs.
                    But she is really very young
            and will think so later.

Now nothing can claim her.
            I am quiet, all chrysalis,
                    hidden in her closet.

New Lincoln Penny

*   *   *   *   *

Now that you're thirty-five and old enough,
why don't you want to be president, Dad?
You're already a lawyer. You don't sluff
off. *I turned the shiny one-center and*

*hit the fishbowl sideways to make the fish
swim fast.* You don't have to be a judge. Please?
Every day you could make many speeches.
Won't you even try? Think of the parties.

The president makes a lot of money
so you could even buy a little farm.
Eisenhower has one, with some donkeys.
Why don't we get a donkey? I heard Mom

say they're clean animals. Siamese kittens
do nothing but eat and poo, like Susu,
Jeannette's new sister. What if mom has twins
this time? The White House has plenty of room.

*I mumble, shy about my fat mother.
Does he hear? The knot of hands on his ribs
rises, falls. He dreams, I tell my brother,
See how the eyeballs twitch under his lids?*

Shell

*   *

They stop while I'm staring at my tongue tip.
Beyond the bandaided windshield dangles
the red Shell sign. Summer beats its single
note on a petunia stained by oil drip;
bolts glitter in the tar, more like fat june bugs
than hardware upended. I cross my legs.

Father's voice floats over me the first time,
then jerks like an old Chevy caught in gear:
"I'm not stopping again." Smearing the rear
window, the grease-streaked attendant scowls. I'm
sure there's only a board over a hole,
chickens, dusty children who look. I roll
my tongue, sink into the vinyl, rehearse
deafness. We pass two rushing brown rivers.

Permission to Live

*   *   *   *   *

Good as any Kennedy, she raised nine
on a farm near silos full of missiles.
We shouted the postwar pledge—*seconds,
please*—and kept our elbows off the table.

Breeding's the only hope, she now maintains,
gung-ho pro-life. I answer: more children
make more fodder for the Weltschmerz laying
of eggs on radiators. No jejune

was Ishi, the last of his tribe. True, sex
for sex exposes not ingenuous
pleasure, but death, the urgent crooning checked,
the twitching cold limbs, the heart motionless.

But why didn't you stop Hiroshima?
You've passed it to me, like a poison coat
in a fairytale. Your silence, Mama,
feeds my anger and the question with it:

what will I say to my child as it snows
that last winter's papery afterglow—
Play in it?

Heartshape

*   *   *

for Shirley

How high the Piper cruised!
How loud the night's elastic
sang! How clear your pilot's
windshielded eyes! Then, in the comfort
of sleep seconds too long,
those broad fields you thought you'd
escaped hit, sparing none.

Rescued once in Africa,
I loved a small plane's
running starts, the unmarked
earth below. Our captain often
slept, set course, slept.
"The worst is marabou.
They fly so fast it doesn't
help to swerve."

In the obituary your child
left no father. You alone
must have sung to her
in that contralto you soloed
with all our choir years,
taught her those high school
cheers, how to wallpaper
with comics. Your father was

no father, the more you had to
please him for. You, brother, child,
pilot—some say lover—flew him
to the playoffs in that private
plane. How you must have loved
"private." You saved
for the fuel, his first ride
anywhere.

He never thanked you,
seldom spoke at all,
except with solemn derision,
all eight of his kids got
by a plumber's hygiene.
You trusted
only your brother,
your girl

baby born to no man,
immaculately conceived
in nine novenas. You'd
forgotten His face, the one
your mother turned to for a while,
then divorced and lost her state
of grace. In Africa
women fall possessed,

recover with prayer only
when apologies and remedies are made.
Your mother changed her name,
even her first. "Didn't want
any sheet cake with Fay
across it." She had the brains
you got, but born penniless,
you stayed broke.

From age eight you worked
to buy her toasters,
matching saucers, avocado
Frigidaires, all to make
her misery less, skipping even
the new dress, your outfits
bursting apart at puberty,
cutting your armpits raw.

Africa didn't get me
and there's no *why* for that
except in its heartshaped whimsy.
After your funeral your family
burst apart, ready as milkweed,
settling like ash plane-rides—apart,
settling like teeth
on impact, everyone asleep.

Carwash Kiss

*   *   *   *

The carnival doesn't rival the carwash.
For a quarter, I could get my brother

to ride on top and come out red as
a letterjacket while the spray steamed

through the window seams, a date's hand
cupped the edge of my Bermudas,

his lips opened on my neck. Then,
as it dripped dry, the doors still locked

so I could say things like *where
next*, my brother would start to holler.

Rite

You're up in the pickup doodling gears,
thinking of your girlfriend's most recent refusal
regarding thighs so fruitlike, so softly haired,
when, looking up, you see the sunset smack the windshield
like some punk band's opening number. To that
you make the tape deck swallow its sandwich, then wriggle
into second as it blasts out the sound
of a boxcar's brakes. It's then, or just about,

given the frozenness of the next minute, that you
clear the driveway and nose left to correct for the corner
and bump over something, a little metal in it,
bad for the chassis, goddammit, Dad won't let you borrow—
You jerk-stop, get out. One glance at the trike's
long red scratch against the paint job slows your walk
and your fingers buzz your goddamn pimples.
                    The kid's

small, stupidly small. When someone's four-door shrieks past,
you try waving it down, but it's you who dislodges
the tiny tennis shoe and take the bundle into your arms,
arms that have held only girls before, and you who blubber
on top of him, not a piece lopped or crushed, then, in panic,
almost drop him, remembering you're never supposed to pick them up,
and, between putting him down and holding him closer,
he opens his eyes and you're in them, over and over,

in identical wonder: How'd I get here? Someone calls,
a high female voice. You curse it, the wide suburban-blank
lawns sloping down into the road, the driveways graded for drainage,
the picture windows modestly and foolishly curtained.
You consider putting him in the cab and letting him steer,
your first fathering, but he spots his trike
and lets loose a shriek which alerts half of the otherwise
somnambulent neighborhood. Thank you

his mother says, as you hand him over. Thank me?
You peer into the dark pavement, answering questions.
You want to turn yourself in, return to someone being
taken care of, locked in your room at least, but
they're all laughing, even your father, who takes
the keys from your shaking hand and like them,
says you're lucky, lucky.

As the Birds

*　　*　　*

I felt very poor that year,
sleeping by the car, under stars,
my child and the lover,
each in their own furrow,
the dirt humped up like gravesites,
and mornings, wetting the ash
in my mouth, and swallowing it,
the price of consciousness.
We were not bums but bathed daily

in a sluice or by some weedy cottonwood
and we never went hungry or I'd still
hear the child calling out in the night,
desperate as a predator. Still,
we had no home, no work to return to.
The trees thickened to forest or
balded to desert while why we drove
became as absurd as those gobbed bloodied gnats
spread on the windshield.

But when the child sang, we sang.
And when he cried, we sang.
No radio told us of tornadoes
nor of what else we'd find (sleep,
food, friends) and when the child
napped on the sticky vinyl, we looked
in this same thicket for love,
as if it had been left for us alone,
under the low leaves.

Once we ducked into an empty farmhouse,
its linoleum buckling with dog's pee,
and found the watchdog himself where
the mice had cleaned him. We didn't
pass by to plump the beds. We'd
forgotten about beds anyway,
and the child hadn't known them,
just breast, just the soft hollow
of my arm, so we stayed on the porch
and the rain kept the light until dawn.

Single Parent Wants to See a Film but Has No Sitter

*   *   *   *   *   *   *   *   *   *

Mom, don't cover my eyes.
The audience turns and titters:
the film's not bad in TV terms.
Still, I try to keep the knife
and the girl and the man
separate. But he lifts my hands:
what is not seen is worse,
a horror adage that always works.

Thank god it's foreign.
I whisper the subtitles
into his ear, changing the words
to match what I think he knows.
Soon popcorn trickles from my hand
to his, he kisses me once
like the couple in front,
and I lose track of the plot.

Until he starts to sob: *the dog
is lost.* We have to leave.
*If it's not real, then what's
it for?* I say picture
after picture flickers by so fast
it's the eye that moves
the movies, that it's all lie.
I don't say why.

Nevermind. He's already mooning
over some plastic space hermaphrodite.
I piggyback him home, wipe his chin
of pizza, and stroke his ivory
and doe-black eyes closed.

It's then I know, my arms around him
and his pillow, that what's on-screen
is just our clumsy rune
to reverse the caveman's magic:
none of this, please, none of it.

My Portrait

*   *   *

Two sets of concentric *o*'s, loose fried eggs,
decorate my chest. He giggles. And legs?
He grips the thick crayon: That's too easy.
And it is. He drags a geode to me.

This is the male part. He points to a nub
of bare amethyst. And if you don't rub
it, it gets dull. Here, under, is the female.
Only in this species are they colorful.

This year he's supposed to ask to marry me.
Then, like all spurned lovers, we're enemies.

Pink

*   *

In China I remembered you only once:
the restaurant's speciality, chosen
from a braid of live varieties,
spiraled to the floor while the waiter
flayed it with a knife flicked

from his wrist. The snake made your initial
over and over the black tile.
What pain! Love's all touch
was the ideogram it made as it crossed
the hot stones to the table.

The Sixties

Every age, like every human body,
has its own distemper.
—*Emerson*

Were we the only ones swimming nude
           under the overpass?
                   Every interchange
in river country engorged you,
triggered musk so thick our clothes
           stuck.

                   And afterward,
sunning on the carhood, if we spoke
           of having children, it was pure praise,
the organs smacking after,
                       not premonition.

Were all those other stops
           at hilltops with overlooks and bushes,
           at roadside parks with hidden tables,
           at empty barns scoured by rats,
                 lanolin-sweet, fertile,

        just the produce
of an era, so many of us solving
               sex over and over,

its sunset flushed

the whole country? Or if I now
        park the child-thick car
              and fight my way into some
mosquito-whining copse,
              will I still find a couple?

His Dark

*   *   *

I

The volume of the dandelion
                 after it is blown
into the blue of the neighbor's yard,
the spikes of grass gunmetal
                 with early dew,
                            is darkness.

After midnight
he may kiss you
if the darkness weighing the flora
                 is sufficient.
                      Then you are wanting transparency,
a higher form of nudity.

Learn the dark
he prods, the reds and blues—
                      the colors
are nothing—
                 half his face
                            so close
         it is featureless.

The buggy heat
      swirls in out of the dark,
its promise
      not in the footsteps blackening
the driveway
but in the fear of too much
   definition:
      "You see what I mean?"

The empty stalk and the colorless wind.
   You can feel your arms open,
        so they must be.

II

The dark models the snow.

                    Its figures,
the carrot-nosed fat man
          and an icicle so curved
it could not be made from water, amuses
                    you, you even
          laugh,
                         but the resemblance . . .

                    The lines
on your forehead
                         are caused by a descent
          of darkness
                    slow as a snow
of feathers,
                    their shadow mottling your clenched
                    now spotting hands.

                    Light is omission, he'd said,
a job undone.

It was the dark that took him away,
                    station after station,
                         into the blanketed starless night.

Blessing

*   *   *

Once in the shower, your sex takes on
mollusk definition and the glass case
is a specimen show. In the mirror,
I pause to admire how my leg creases
my hip in a fortune-cookie bend.
Inside, maybe the cells mix.

The steam posits a dream, which is,
after all, what the past is.
Last night, in bed, I heard
the shaver and my father
stepped into the light.
Why would anyone shave naked?
Shock secured that child's puzzle.

Until, a moment later, you
came to me, soft-faced,
astringent, all skin and mouth,
yes, as others have done, yes.
But you alone delivered me
the answer, the one in which
I am my mother and I do this

and this and this. Steam
makes our lips slide. I say:
women prefer a higher heat;
you pass the soap under
my folded breast. Confidence
rises between us.

Night Sail

*　　*　　*

A rare cloud covering the whole
of the moon, or the dog on its hindlegs, howling?
　　Who cares—I'm awake, and alone. It's so quiet

　the dream is the water at the windowsill
　　and the darkness that plaits it
　　　the hair of Greek women,
　　　　　　　thick, black, curled
　　　　　with connotation, the usual wailing.

　　　　I fear, and the accursed windchimes
barely chime.
　　　　　I'm even inclined to cry. How easily
the bay would take its rearing prey, one black wind
　　　snapping the mast—
　　　　　　　you'd left at nine.

　The buoys strain, a tinkling
　　　　that gives up nothing. If the earth's round,
my love's still here, somewhere.

So I hear what I want,
i.e., the widow's walk wasn't put up
    for consolation. But there's nothing there,
        a disquieting stillness in the air.
    I find the door,
    my nude length gliding out like milkweed
      or any other blossom
        gone unheeded.

    Each plank in the yacht club's boardwalk
  receives me musically. If I hit three at once
will the chord be Dorian? I can't fuss.
    If some drunk
      boatsman should roll over and see—

    It is cold, and getting colder but I don't retreat.
I stare at the lapping water, its so-landlocked
      gibberish. It's the wind I'm after,
  its overture: *return, return, return.*
    If only some triangle
      would blot out the stars,
          or a dusting of oars . . .

Dumb Husband

*   *   *   *

As the right brain twines around the left
and forgets it
                    so
                              Sepulvida takes several turns
            and we lose the thread of it,
our adult exchange, for once not money-based
    or in the liturgy of children,
              whatever it was, lost at
                        the first unfamiliar interchange.

Beaches, palms, 7-11, a corridor
  of thick brick stoops,
            the level is now Yes or No
and a nervous stomping on the gas
                              pedal.

            I drive. There are worlds to miss
      if you're always right,
the only argument for travel,
            true adventure. Look at it this way.

            You look at it this way.

A semi does not. Its lower tones
      reach our children's bones and a sorrow
links us all, the crabby baby,
      the boy pillowed in comics,
                       me
turning off
      then on again.

    You rattle the map
        with a flair for forgiveness
    saying It's true,
        I never talk to you.

Spiders

*   *   *

It's so cold the kid's
boots don't track in,
snow appears on threads

without falling. I read
about a talking spider, no
mean embalmer.

Glancing forward, I remember
she dies. It was the first time
I cried, reading. "So?" I pull

his brother's pajamas over
his knobbed shoulders, the brother
who's only photos

and a gold chocolate bunny
now. "I think I'll build
a snowman tomorrow."

*

*A word is elegy to what
it signifies.* Guilt rocks
on its prongs, tight

to the marrow of sorrow.
I have a headache
and turning down the light

I see a daddylonglegs
parading its harmless, webless self
across the davenport.

Natural death's an anachronism.
I'm reminded of someone who,
making love, cried "more"

the whole time until there was
no more. The spider has no caution,
or it's all forgotten.

*

I'm reading African songs
when the phone rings. The songs
are not as elegant as the masks

but still there's business:
the lion who never grows feeble,
a fabulous sorceress. The news

is a crib death, the baby
stone cold this morning.
I know shock, grief, loss.

I've paid mine to say those words
of simple consolation:
I'm alive. Bantu don't name

their children until they walk.
I close my book, turn off
the light. Straight from

myself I've inherited
my moment of eloquence
in this cold, lousy dark.

*

Sex, sex, sex, Whitman's inverse,
the sibilance of helpless lust.
I tell the bereaved to touch.

*

Who sleeps but children?
I listen to the mice fight
in the broiler, for once

a welcome furor. It means
the poison's gone, no more dead
in the walls. And another bump:

the cat playing with the spiders.
I bless them all, I sleep,
going bean-size inside my mother.

Woman with Happiness inside Her

*   *   *   *   *   *   *

—literal translation of the Chinese figure for pregnancy

The grizzly scanning the washout
and her cub
make one unit.
They go for the slight blue flowers
under the red-yellow-grey
of the sumac's fall,
for where there's color . . .
The paws, wound as if bandaged
with the gauze of cold honey . . .
The bees, percussion
to pleasure . . .

*

Detumescence comes slowly
to my sex.
Life's charge—
a little dash in the sky,
space hurtling through space
headed for the boom, the gyroscope
swinging and tilting more and more
fancy.

He slides into me again,
the only taboo, procreation.
It excites us; our couplings
go perverse,
the seed pooled
at the navel.

Every time my flow's late,
I take stock of the vessel,
the pod and the chancre,
the open pit and the tree
with its suitable shade

and I sing below it, below
the bough that is always breaking,
singing to the cradle that swings way out
over the heartbeat,
over the grave.

*

Nothing is premature.
What we light
is the infant's eye.
It catches like a match
against a zipper.

Meeting this eye,
we empty into it,
the Möbius of chemistry
burning down,
burning.

And it changes as we watch
from toad to sea anemone,
the fingerbone lengthening,
pointing. It knows
exactly who to blame.

The child who fell
on his head and opened
his eyes
and tried to talk
and the one who kicked
out of me and kicks still
and the one who kept
his girdle of knotted flesh
and had no sex,
no fishy grasp
at all—who's left?

*

In Africa, where we began,
a hot wind dries the swelling
woman's breasts,
the milk of one,
the tears of another.

*

For answers, I make
my only outing: the crèche
of the city, the wise men lined up
with their gifts,
the shepherds and the sheep,
even the angels swinging on secular straps.
In the city's vortex,
the manger empties of rats
so quickly it's as if they know
about kings
and their concomitant
responsibility.

Death is the gift I'd give it.
Why have another if the world's
about to blow? Death is the gift
I'd give it, the cantor's cry,
one plague or another.

I apply balm,
soak the child in vitamins
and minerals and he shoots
(only at targets, at animals,
for food) practicing his screendeath
which seems invitation to me,
each gunned-down
soldier with a mother,
each dam planted between
cub and the club.

*

What the skaters believe is solid
thins, its *o* pulses.
From inside that well, the fontanelle,
a single note deepens,
deafens.

*

It is time to wish for
the hotel room
where children are made and unmade,
though now coathangers hang immovable
in the closets. The lights
crossing the ceiling *x* out my previous life.
How to duck those *x*'s, that light,
and enter what we forget, the soul,
the body turned inside out, the seam showing,
the labels proclaiming
to whom we owe.

*

In India, Kali waves her every limb,
every orifice
open, howling. This
is what is feared: the power
of Saturn salting the children,
every awful organ
in balance.

*

Out of my mother,
crying on the kitchen table,
her spoon dripping offal to the clean floor,
all nine of us. We're penitent,
making her cry more,
making her wish her tears would either
well us away or clean us whole,
without undressing.
A full belly to us
was something else to her.

Now my own row of little boots
seek the toes
for one more pre-potty dance
and tiny ratty mittens clap their dust.
I am that age, hers,
when she had me.
How can I refuse . . .

I fear the vessel cracking.
Women go crazy from it,
and I am crazy when the body takes over,
one moosecall away from delivery,
the petit mort so much more than
the gasp and the sigh.

*

Nothing is premature.
Biology sweeps over the one
who is reading, studying
under the fresh-lit lamp
of herself; it is the cunning biology
of joy and she puts the book down.
She will have it.

Yes, it will be yes.
The swollen breast heaves
and the banner's
lifted willfully, if not
willingly.

Then, despite the self buried
and the decision as filleted
and dried as any god's, the cusp of myself
announces reversal, the thrum
of my blood only, the goat desires,
desires only.

To that, the ecru slip folds
to the floor and a musk of breasts
steams from the pockets.
The bear takes it up
and dances in it,
her brief estrus simple:
a sumac tryst,
a cub each year
in the washout.
That flame we light
to scare her off
is our only cautery.

The Needle with Both Hands

*   *   *   *   *   *

Always fatal, Tay-Sachs disease affects only Eastern European children.

for R. N. B.

Over the waves of his chest,
you watch the sun go up, again. How
accidentally the birds cross it!
How seemingly accidental.

What random choices led you
to him—your darling
from the same steppes
as Zhivago's, and your own.

Then he's dressed, and you're almost.
Leaning over, he pulls your slip up
to put his hand over that fat part of you,
where swims the swimmer. Enter
                         Tay and Sachs,

two men good at identifying
    a certain kind of certain death
       due to a certain mix of genes
          of children with certain parents.

Today you go to determine your chances,
rather, its chances,
all euphemism unable to cover
the chance red spot on the growing retina.

After your doctor has his way,
you can see on the screen
the little swimmer trying to escape,
holding the needle with both hands,

                         just reflex.

              The verdict
takes time to swell and ripen.
The doctor offers his only balm, a curse:
knowledge without antidote. All you know

is that the immortals throw no bones,
that you inherit nothing
but genes and bravery, both faltering.
You trot back

to work and your new belly
swirls with the fetal pig you took the eyes from,
grade ten. To market, to market.
You pull your goddamn shrinking coat

around you. Nothing like
the stir of life that has no chance.
You shrug. It's only the size of your finger,
you don't care—

             But knowing at the end
of ten hours' pitched screaming,
your insides reversing, you get

                  nothing—

Does it make sounds yet?
You know all about life.
You majored in biology, pirouetted
through the wedding night.

What goes where with death?
Choose happiness, you tell your husband,
but accept the truth: the child might die. Suffer and die.
In the three-week wait you type

and each hammer moves the days along.
Waiting, every word from everyone hurts,
every Good Day, careless or concerned,
every word. The only sympathy you want

is the same cruelty shared, all else
grates; for inside, it spins—in fear?
What you must swallow
is the sugar cube of your continuing,

the inescapable desire to pee
that stirs you mornings, hours before dawn.
But if, at the end of these weeks of waiting,
the white-masked priests come back bearing

no news, which is their best,
you will have brushed off death,
rimed him bright and acceptable
and seen it slant.

Either way. That is, what happens
doesn't matter. You eat.
You lie down. The sun shrinks.
The daily din you're thankful for

rescinds its paper currency that nothing backs up.
Your husband puts on a pot to boil, and another.
He can't feel it inside, though he's eaten the same
sour apple. It has only his genes,

the underclothes, the bra,
the brief of the body. You are dumb before
his helplessness. The cord to belly to cord
will not be broken,

ripped untimely as it may be.
"Mamma" has happened
and the rockinghorse of your heart
will heave on.

Both in and out of the Game and Watching and Wondering at It

*   *   *   *   *   *   *

for Scott Giantvalley

Over the convalescents' patio
something peels,
either eucalyptus or smog-seared palm,
and you brush it
from your bedjacket with a flourish
from your schoolboy days,
when to train a daddylonglegs
up a girl's dress
wasn't for secondhand titillation
or torture
but to vamp the eek!

Looking up into the usual blue,
the everyday, nothing's-wrong blue,
you recall another outdoors,
your wedding, mother weeping—
you saw that tear—
when you pricked your finger and put it over his
to seal it,
the only boy-on-boy ceremony.
The same old blood! the same red-running blood!

It's okay, Dad, you wrote last week,
        forget that wages-of-sin chagrin,
no point punching out that kind of friend.
                In LA, you tell him, sometimes
                        ferns spring up
out of the mulching fossils
                in the middle of the sidewalk,
        aberrant, luxuriant, still landscape.

    You decide to die in one of those decorator malls,
the Mercedes circling, honking, trumpeting
        to get at your parking,
                or at the beach,
blistering on one side, fish-white the other, steps
        from the musclemen and your mate
who allows you
        the dignity.

                You steady the leaves. The sun—
        there it goes—
    promises nothing.

            Day is done,
                as in Scouts, that travesty,
and into his beard you go,
                divine inside and out,
        still shameless,
and as weak
        as the laving ocean.

Betty's Silence

*　　*　　*　　*

for Elizabeth Kray

The six white roses she set quietly
at the nurses' station surprised Shirley
so much she burst into tears. "Oh, Betty,
you shouldn't have . . . What this means to me . . ."
Ditto, Betty went: *No more therapy*
for two months and maybe remission. Be
well yourself. Don't let the head nurse torture you
into a robot like her, continue
your laying on of hands, how you pat mine
into place as if to ward off unkind
rays. Just the sight of your hips, those bulwarks
matching the famed Willendorf matriarch
but nonetheless life, make me smile. I'll miss
you. But Betty had tears herself. "What, these?"

Miracles

*　　*　　*

A miracle in fact means work.
—Weldon Kees

       Three ladies
             run their Toyota
         into the intersection against
the light.
       One grey head-stalk sways out
       as if checking the tires
              and shatters the window

         as the young man's sportscar
skids into them.

       Standing in the glass she pats her hair
          and refuses
an ambulance. She wants "To get that boy . . ."

       And exhaust smokes around her.

When something sweetens that part
which we grasp toward,
that patch of light that outlines
the masks on the wall
for no good reason,
the cavern bursting
out of
the cave's beleaguering twists,

concealment's required:
                    The Millionaire in silhouette,
                    never bemused or pitying,
his couriers as surreptitious
as melting ice,

                    yet the message must be as obvious
as a grocery label
because there are those we miss—
                    day and night,
                    meteorites fall all around us.
And if hypochondria is a wished-for disease
                    and the accident-prone are disturbed,
there are some who tend to miracle.

In a San Diego tract town
when crosses appear
on the bathroom walls—
I paid no attention to it,
before the reporters—
the miracle's like beauty
apprehended through a picture window,
attributed to pollution
and the house being set so
on the plot.

At most we're witnesses:
In Giotto's *Annunciation*
we're the disembodied hands
that arrow down to the groveling husband,
God about to cuckold him,
       the saint/wife bent in prayer,
           ecstatic against
the electric blue background,
      just enough wind
         against her garments
to suggest *mistral*,

                  what drove Van Gogh to his ear,

a Mediterranean persistence
that seeds the most barren
      and topples the fertile.

But we can't hear the message,
the whatfor, the whisper.
Sex, you'd think, would tune us in.
        Life we can pull out of test tubes
but you touch me there
and we're talking transport,
a tapping
        of something bigger,
like Ben Franklin, his kite,
    his key,
the swami beckoning
the devotee,
     needing her
to complete the arc.

And that first kiss recalls
that first kiss, mother's,
father's, Hans
with the milk-lined forelip,
         all stupidly romantic,
yes, highly colored by cinema-love
or bookish adultery
         (the notepaper floating from the carriage)
yet evolving straight from
                  some proto-moment
essential to the species, beyond the yawn
         of Olduvai.

If that's not miraculous enough,
there's inspiration:
         the genius of glass
set in the holes of our houses,
         the grooved disc full of music,
         the iamb.
But inspiration's been relegated
         to the unconscious,
                  the winged chariot bumping forward
in half-sleep,
         the famous circle
of snakes forming benzene by themselves,
         visions
just certain motes against certain light,
         inspiration more breath
than what keeps us
                  from whirling apart.
         It's a comfort, not to believe more.

Why should we go down
on our knees
when it's our knees
we want to worship?

We stand at the mountaintop
and shout
who, who, who
for the Cartesian echo,

                the truth of Narcissus
that we are not water,
                the lie of the tombstone
that it returns us,
                molecule by molecule,

compels us to circle
                the bulbed models,
the mated salts.
        We have science clutched to our breast
like a lily,
                we are the Pharaoh
        laid in the most propitious
                      shaft of starlight.
        We believe the waterfall's
stopped
                because a little girl
sits on the stream
or that Guadeloupe's church
                    protrudes from the lava
because that's what's tallest.
        Science, the ultimate Narcissus:
what we see is all there is.

But then it happens:
What do you want,
the doctors shout without opening their mouths,
        a miracle?
              We're dumb too,
for the child
is dying,
is dead,
             a small, slight body
trapped in the lower lefthand corner
of this bare green room
while the EEG tickertapes triumphant
arrival elsewhere,
             binds
what's left behind.

Three days pass. They always do.
We start to think
the Pied Piper can't get them all,
          his tune falters—surely we were
       thankful enough, a child's
that kind of miracle.

But the stone is all we have of sanity.
       We don't want it pushed back,
the corpse coming unwrapped,
dream-naked, terrified.

No. The miracle must be a little bell
in the back garden, coming out of silence,
not the gong
that sets us tumbling.

Notes

*　　*

The line *A word is elegy to what it signifies* in "Spiders" is from "Meditation at Lagunitas" by Robert Hass.

The title of "Both in and out of the Game and Watching and Wondering at It" is taken from Whitman's "Song of Myself," part 4. The line *The same old blood! the same red-running blood!* is from his "I Sing the Body Electric."

The Iowa Poetry Prize Winners

*   *   *   *   *   *   *

1987
Elton Glaser, *Tropical Depressions*
Michael Pettit, *Cardinal Points*

1988
Mary Ruefle, *The Adamant*
Bill Knott, *Outremer*

1989
Terese Svoboda, *Laughing Africa*
Conrad Hilberry, *Sorting the Smoke*